# INCOMPLETE

*Life through the Eyes of a Small-Town Pastor*

Shawn LaRue

Copyright © 2017 Shawn LaRue.

All rights reserved. No part of this book may be used or reproduced by any means, graphic, electronic, or mechanical, including photocopying, recording, taping or by any information storage retrieval system without the written permission of the author except in the case of brief quotations embodied in critical articles and reviews.

Scripture quotations marked NRSV are taken from the New Revised Standard Version of the Bible, Copyright 1989, by the Division of Christian Education of the National Council of the Churches of Christ in the United States of America. Used by permission. All rights reserved.

Scripture quotations marked RSV are taken from the Revised Standard Version of the Bible, copyright 1946, 1952, 1971 by the Division of Christian Education of the National Council of the Churches of Christ in the USA. Used by permission.

Scripture quotations marked NLT are taken from the Holy Bible, New Living Translation, copyright 1996, 2004, 2007. Used by permission of Tyndale House Publishers, Inc. Carol Stream, Illinois 60188. All rights reserved.

WestBow Press books may be ordered through booksellers or by contacting:

WestBow Press
A Division of Thomas Nelson & Zondervan
1663 Liberty Drive
Bloomington, IN 47403
www.westbowpress.com
1 (866) 928-1240

Because of the dynamic nature of the Internet, any web addresses or links contained in this book may have changed since publication and may no longer be valid. The views expressed in this work are solely those of the author and do not necessarily reflect the views of the publisher, and the publisher hereby disclaims any responsibility for them.

Any people depicted in stock imagery provided by Thinkstock are models, and such images are being used for illustrative purposes only. Certain stock imagery © Thinkstock.

ISBN: 978-1-5127-7728-4 (sc)
ISBN: 978-1-5127-7729-1 (hc)
ISBN: 978-1-5127-7727-7 (e)

Library of Congress Control Number: 2017902980

Print information available on the last page.

WestBow Press rev. date: 3/02/2017

Dedication

To Traci, Adam, and Grant

# CONTENTS

Preface ..................................................................................... xi

Chapter 1   The apostle Paul tells us how we are called to love .................................................................................. 1

Chapter 2   The gift of being fully present ..................... 3

Chapter 3   The condition of the heart ......................... 5

Chapter 4   We serve a God of love ............................... 7

Chapter 5   Christ reveals to those who have faith ................... 9

Chapter 6   When the material things of this world don't deliver ............................................................................... 11

Chapter 7   The elusive gift of peace ........................... 13

Chapter 8   The abundant life of faith ......................... 15

Chapter 9   The gift of doubt, the stone that sharpens the blade of faith ............................................................ 17

Chapter 10  The closer we draw to Christ, the more we are able to love .................................................................. 19

Chapter 11  Those who love me will keep my word .............. 21

Chapter 12  Knowing instead of judging .................................. 23

Chapter 13  Love cancels out fear ........................................... 25

Chapter 14  I'm too busy and I don't have time ...................... 27

Chapter 15  The worst kind of lost ........................................... 29

Chapter 16  The meaningless pursuit of titles ......................... 31

Chapter 17  Many talents, one body ....................................... 33

Chapter 18  Our most authentic self is found in Christ ......... 35

Chapter 19  Everything starts with prayer .............................. 37

Chapter 20  Making it right ...................................................... 39

Chapter 21  The proof of the resurrection ...............................41

Chapter 22  Place your trust in God ........................................ 43

Chapter 23  We must take time to pray to meet the demands of this life ............................................................... 45

Chapter 24  Faith calls us to sacrifice ...................................... 47

Chapter 25  To whom have you shown mercy? ..................... 49

Chapter 26  What will become of the church? ....................... 51

Chapter 27  Are you Mary or Martha? .................................... 53

Chapter 28  Father, holy and blessed be thy name ................ 55

Chapter 29  Every day is a battle ............................................. 57

Chapter 30  We remember those who gave ............................ 59

Chapter 31  You are first and foremost a child of God ......... 61

Chapter 32  We serve a big God .................................................. 63

Chapter 33  How will your story of faith read? ....................... 65

Chapter 34  God prepares us while we wait .......................... 67

Chapter 35  Earth or eternity, convenience or Christ ............ 69

Chapter 36  Immanuel, God with us ........................................ 71

Chapter 37  Faith, family, and forgiveness .............................. 73

Chapter 38  Restoration and healing ....................................... 75

Chapter 39  Listening to our lives ............................................. 77

Chapter 40  Doing for those who can't do anything for us . 79

Chapter 41  Suffering gives us a choice .................................. 81

Chapter 42  Prayer works, and God still listens ..................... 83

Chapter 43  Our guilt, Christ's sacrifice ................................... 85

Chapter 44  The heart of discipleship ..................................... 87

Chapter 45  Surrender ............................................................... 89

Chapter 46  I want, I want ......................................................... 91

Chapter 47  The wages of sin ................................................... 93

Chapter 48  The word became flesh ....................................... 95

Chapter 49  The danger of judging others ............................. 97

Chapter 50  Do we know how to suffer? ................................. 99

Chapter 51  Offering ourselves as a living sacrifice ............ 101

Chapter 52  Coming before God with empty hands and an open heart ................................................................. 103

Chapter 53  Those with hearts of faith grieve ................. 105

Chapter 54  Blessed are those who are humble ................ 107

Chapter 55  Those who pursue holiness ........................... 109

Chapter 56  No one exists outside God's mercy and grace 111

Chapter 57  Christ convicts us of our sin ........................ 113

Chapter 58  Sins of the heart ........................................... 115

Chapter 59  Getting comfortable in our own skin ............ 117

Chapter 60  Reaching in Christ's direction ..................... 119

Chapter 61  Anything but weak ....................................... 121

Chapter 62  Take up your cross, deny yourself, and follow me ................................................................... 123

Chapter 63  A childlike faith ........................................... 125

About the Author .............................................................. 131

# PREFACE

My reason for writing this book is similar to the call I experienced to ministry. Despite not having the credentials to do it, I just felt that was the direction in which I was being led. Shortly after being assigned as a lay minister to Seymour United Methodist Church (UMC) in Seymour, Iowa, I started writing short devotionals for the local newspaper. I had thoughts of trying to put those devotionals into a book, but I would quickly dismiss them. But such thoughts continued and ultimately ended with multiple conversations with Gretchen Keene at WestBow.

I am now appointed as a local licensed pastor at Seymour UMC. At one of the classes I've taken along the way, an instructor said that all of us are incomplete. The statement was not meant to be derogatory or offensive. It was true. It was something that I needed to hear. I needed to be told that I am incomplete and that it is okay. I needed permission.

I needed to be told that my past failures do not define me. I needed to be told that we are incomplete and that we can begin to find completeness only with God, with Christ, and through his sacrifice on the cross. We all need to be reminded that we are incomplete, which is okay. We are all works in progress. This is not an excuse to go and sin some more, but an affirmation of our brokenness.

Although short on ministry credentials, I've read and studied enough to know that God forgives us, redeems us, and begins his holy work with us. Knowing that wasn't enough. I needed to hear it from another person. Maybe you need to hear it too. If we were created complete, we wouldn't see our need for God. I hope that what I have written will add to your spiritual journey.

To those who have guided me on my spiritual journey, thank you.

# 1

# The apostle Paul tells us how we are called to love

Love is patient; love is kind; love is not envious or boastful or arrogant or rude. It does not insist on its own way; it is not irritable or resentful; it does not rejoice in wrongdoing, but rejoices in the truth. It bears all things, believes all things, hopes all things, endures all things.

—1 Corinthians 13:4–7

In order to love, you must offer your heart to someone else with the knowledge that there is nothing more precious you can offer. You must reveal all your faults, flaws, shortcomings, and things you don't like about yourself. Being vulnerable is difficult and something most of us go to great lengths to avoid. When we weep, we often run for cover, not wanting others to see us that way.

Love is risky and dangerous. Love can say no, turn its back, and walk away. That story belongs to many; it is our story. It happened in the garden of Eden. Adam and Eve turned from God and disobeyed. They had everything except for one thing, and they couldn't resist. The ugliness of sin and the endless desires of the flesh take our focus from God. But it is God to whom we must return.

There is risk in love. But it is precisely what we are called to do, what we were made to do. Those intense feelings about those close to us give us a glimpse of what heaven will be like.

# 2
## The gift of being fully present

When the wine gave out, the mother of Jesus said to him, "They have no wine." And Jesus said to her, "How does that concern you and me? My hour has not yet come."

—John 2:34

What was Christ's first miracle? It wasn't healing or raising someone from the dead. It was turning water into wine. Christ, at his mother's request and somewhat reluctantly, saved the host of the wedding feast considerable embarrassment.

Jesus proved he has dominion over time and space, growth, water and wine. His first miracle was about celebration and fellowship. The wedding feast could have gone on for days. In today's world, where time has become the most precious commodity, this miracle is about spending time with family and friends in celebration.

The world today prizes speed and efficiency. If we're not careful, this can bleed into our relationships, leaving us feeling isolated and alone. Leaving us little joy.

I struggle with experiencing joy far too little. I steal it from myself. I think that once I clear this hurdle, pay off this bill, or get a different job, somehow I will be happier. It doesn't work. The first miracle is a celebration and about living in the moment. Don't take, steal, or delay your joy.

# 3
# The condition of the heart

A certain ruler asked him, "Good teacher, what must I do get inherit eternal life?" Jesus said to him, "Why do you call me good? No one is good but God alone."

—Luke 18:18–19

"What should I do to get eternal life?" asks a young, wealthy man of Christ. Do you think this young man was concerned with the well-being of his soul, or did he have wisdom beyond his years? Had it occurred to him that eternal life could not be purchased?

Do you believe sin became part of our story, and God has done everything he can to fix it? Do you believe that Christ came to this world to save us? Do you believe eternal life can't be earned, purchased, or bartered for?

True belief brings good works and acts of service. From belief comes obedience, freedom, and joy. What does each of us have to do to inherit eternal life? Believe.

# 4

# We serve a God of love

God did not send the Son into the world to condemn the world, but in order that the world might be saved through him.

—John 3:17

I can talk about Jesus, and you can read about him, but who is he to you? Who is this poor carpenter from Nazareth?

God has worked tirelessly ever since Adam and Eve's transgression in the garden of Eden. He sent kings, prophets, a pillar of fire by night, and a cloud by day. Still a gap existed between him and us. So what did he do?

He sent his son, his one and only. Can you imagine making such a sacrifice? He sent Christ, fully human yet fully divine, so he could relate to all the things we have to deal with—fear, rejection, frustration, temptation, and the list goes on. He loves us without conditions, without basis on anything we can do. Just because we are. He was obedient to the point of death. It was obedience to his father that held Jesus to the cross; it wasn't the nails.

Christ loved unconditionally, but it seems like I rarely do. I have attached my standards to people and measured their worth by it. If I have more money, education, nicer clothes, and a newer car—I win. But I don't win—I lose. I take humanity from others that wasn't mine to take. I didn't love without conditions. I didn't love at all.

Thank God for Jesus, born with the frailty of a child, who grew into a man and saved us from death. Take time to thank God for all that he has done.

# 5

# Christ reveals to those who have faith

Jesus took with him Peter and James and his brother John and led them up a high mountain, by themselves. And he was transfigured before them, and his face shone like the sun, and his clothes became dazzling white. Suddenly there appeared to them Moses and Elijah, talking with him.

—Matthew 17:1–3

Transfiguration. As he often did, Christ set out to pray, but this time he took Peter, James, and John with him. Moses and Elijah appeared and began speaking of how Christ was about to fulfill God's plan. Christ humbled himself in prayer often. Prayer transfigures; it changes the heart. It enlarges it, glorifies God, and brings joy and peace. The power of prayer cannot be underestimated.

In this example, the appearance of Christ's face changed and his clothing became dazzling white. Moses's face shined brightly after encountering God, as ours do too. When we embrace our brokenness, confess our sin, and repent, we find that image of the Creator, which dwells within each of us.

It is when we come to know God that the knowledge of ourselves increases. The depths of our souls can be known. The more we know God, the more we know ourselves, and find our most genuine, authentic self. We are transformed, we are transfigured.

# 6
## When the material things of this world don't deliver

There was a man who had two sons. The younger of them said to his father, "Father, give me the share of the property that will belong to me." So he divided his property between them. A few days later the younger son gathered all he had and traveled to a distant country and there he squandered his property in dissolute living.

—Luke 15:11–13

I see myself in the parable of the prodigal son, and maybe you do too. He was young, and brash, with a desire to live life in the fast lane. He couldn't wait for his father to pass. He needed his inheritance now.

After his father grants his wish, the young man packs his belongings and heads to a distant land. He squanders his money on fast living. He hits bottom, so much so that he asks a farmer to hire him to help with his pigs. He is so hungry that what the pigs are eating looks good to him.

Many of us haven't sunk to this level physically, but how about spiritually? It is when we are at our weakest, hungriest, coldest, and in terrible pain that we cry out to God for mercy. The prodigal son returns home and begs for forgiveness. His father waits for his return and rejoices when it happens. Much the same way our heavenly father rejoices when we return to him, he forgives us of our disobedience.

When living out all the desires of the flesh falls short, when you can't find joy or happiness, turn to God.

# 7
# The elusive gift of peace

When it was evening on that day, the first day of the week, and the doors of the house where the disciples had met were locked for fear of the Jews, Jesus came and stood among them and said, "Peace be with you."

—John 20:19–20

Christ had gone to the cross and died. His followers were dejected and distraught. He died to save us and conquer our fear of death. The disciples were without their leader and met behind closed doors for their own safety.

This is when the resurrected Christ appears among them and says, "Peace be with you." When was the last time you experienced the same? You probably weren't huddled in a locked room in Jerusalem, but when was the last time you were in a desperate place and it was then that you were reminded of or felt God's presence?

It could be a well-timed visitor, phone call, or card—or a passage from the Bible. We serve a big God. We serve a God so big that he died in our place to take away the stain of sin. He tasted death so that we wouldn't have to. That alone should bring us peace.

# 8
# The abundant life of faith

Christ said, "Put out your nets into the deep water and let them down for a catch." Simon replied, "Master, we have worked all night long but have caught nothing. Yet if you say so, I will let down the nets." When they had done this, they caught so many fish that their nets were beginning to break.

—Luke 5:4–6

The disciples were fishing in the Sea of Galilee. They were seasoned, professional fishermen, but they hadn't caught anything all night.

Christ tells them to cast their nets one more time. And doing so, at Christ's direction, they catch more fish than they can pull into the boat. This is how it works with faith, when Christ speaks and we obey.

When we don't see or listen to him, things are empty and bleak. But with his counsel and guidance, our lives are richer and fuller than we could ever imagine.

There is a life that overflows with life. It isn't found in the things of this world—money, possessions, and titles. It is found when our spiritual life comes to life. Our lives make sense only within the framework of faith. Without it, we are just random people living lives without purpose. We are so much more than that.

# 9

# The gift of doubt, the stone that sharpens the blade of faith

But Thomas, one of the twelve, was not with them when Jesus came. So the other disciples told him, "We have seen the Lord." But he said to them, "Unless I see the mark of the nails in his hands, and put my finger in the mark of the nails and my hand in his side, I will not believe."

—John 20:24–25

Doubt. Why is doubt so plentiful and easy to come by?

I have put God on trial many times for things I think he should have done. Where were you, Messiah, when my spouse asked for a divorce, when I lost a loved one, or when my health failed?

It is easy to discount the blessings and focus on the small areas in our life that trouble us. A 98 percent grade in the classroom by our children is outstanding, but it isn't for God. At times we allow the 2 percent we don't like to discount everything that is good about our existence. That way of thinking can create doubt and cause us to give up ground in our spiritual life.

How fortunate are we to serve a merciful and forgiving God when we take our blessings for granted? We can question God, get mad at him, doubt him, stumble and fall, and we still belong to him. We can say how we deserved better and submit a list of demands. Doesn't matter, we've been set aside. No one can take us from him.

# 10

## The closer we draw to Christ, the more we are able to love

This is my commandment, that you love one another as I have loved you. No one has greater love than this, to lay down one's life for one's friends.

—John 15:12

"So now," Christ says, "I am giving a new commandment. Love each other. Just as I have loved you, you should love one another."

Love your neighbor … Okay.

Love the Lord your God with all your heart, mind, and soul … I'll try.

Love others like Christ loves you. Are you crazy? I can try to love people who look, talk, and dress like me, and people who share my values. But sacrifice like Christ did? Sacrifice and be selfless (at times) for those close to me? Sure. But would I sacrifice like Christ did, for people who don't have the same color of skin or background, or for those who can't do anything to benefit me? That is the test.

Through this thing called life, we are called to a deeper knowledge of our God. As this relationship deepens, attachments to this world don't burn as brightly. God is always calling us into a deeper relationship with him, to become more like him. We need to do our part by reading his work, praying, and being part of a community of faith.

Unconditional love, agape love, is the highest form of love. Christ-like love. That is the kind of love to which we are called.

# 11

# Those who love me will keep my word

Judas said to Christ, "Lord, how is it that you will reveal yourself to us, and not to the world?" Jesus answered him, "Those who love me will keep my word, and we will come to them and make our home with them."

—John 14:22–23

"All those who love me will do what I say. My Father will love them, and we will come to them and live with them."

This is Christ's response to a question asked by one of his disciples.

As complicated as I like to make matters of faith, and with all the reading and head knowledge I've attempted to gain, there is nothing like the simplicity of faith. The beauty of God's creation on a crisp fall day. The joy we experience at the birth of a child.

All those who love me will do what I say. All those who come to faith will do what I say. All those who have been convicted of their sin will do as I say.

It's those who see through eyes of faith who truly see Christ and will know him forever. We have to keep Christ's commands, but when we have him in our hearts and minds, it's not difficult to do. Because they have followed my commands, because they are humble, loving, and charitable, because they have responded to God's work and pursuit in their lives.

For those reasons and many more, they will enjoy God's presence in this life and the life to come.

# 12
Knowing instead of judging

And a woman in the city, who was a sinner, having learned that he was eating in the Pharisee's house, brought an alabaster jar of ointment. She stood behind him at his feet, weeping, and began to bathe his feet with her tears and to dry them with her hair. Then she continued kissing his feet and anointing them with the ointment.

—Luke 7:37–38

A Pharisee invites Christ to his home. A woman of the city shows up with a gift for Christ. Who has more faith? The learned man of Scripture or the woman at Christ's feet anointing him with ointment and her tears?

I wish I had the boldness of this woman's faith. Unfortunately, I'm more often like the Pharisee, looking down on her in judgment.

Judging people is easy, but loving them is far more difficult. It takes that precious resource of time. I have judged people without spending a minute with them. They drive too slowly, they live in a run-down house, they don't have nice clothes, and they don't go to church. I ask myself, "What is wrong with them?" No, what is wrong with me?

If we knew the stories of those with whom we cross paths, if we truly knew them, we would be far less apt to pass judgment on them.

# 13

# Love cancels out fear

Epiphany is more than a season or a Sunday at church. Epiphany is a Christian feast celebrating the divine nature of Christ to the Gentiles. Have you experienced an epiphany, a sudden realization or awareness of God's presence in your life?

We all have experiences, revelations, or epiphanies, when things are revealed to us. I read in Henri Nouwen's book *The Inner Voice of Love* that when love ends, fear begins. In the absence of love, you get fear.

How had this not occurred to me before? When we turn from God, who is love, we fall into the traps of the flesh—loneliness, anxiety, fear, greed, jealousy, and so on.

Most of what we do is motivated by either love or fear. Fear of rejection, abandonment, failure, not being liked, or what others will think of us, and not being accepted for who we are. Love cancels out fear.

We were not created to be timid, fearful souls. We were created to be bold, courageous, humble, and loving, in the image of the Creator.

# 14

## I'm too busy and I don't have time

No one can serve two masters; for a slave will either hate the one and love the other, or be devoted to one and despise the other. You cannot serve God and wealth.

—Matthew 6:24

No one can serve two masters, for you will love one and hate the other. Christ talked about money a lot. He probably knew that it was his primary competitor.

The world screams at us with the things it has to offer—fancy vehicles, clothes, phones, places to visit, and things to do. We are told that we can live richer and fuller lives by having and doing more. A whirlwind of activity ensues.

"I'm too busy" is a common catchphrase—too busy to help, too busy to volunteer, too busy to go to church.

"I'm too busy" translated means I don't have my priorities in the proper order and I'm selfish with my time.

Each day is a brand-new opportunity to choose eternity over things of this earth, to pick Christ over convenience. God has given each of us the gift and miracle of life, as difficult and complex as life can be at times. God gives, and gives, and gives some more.

When we embrace the knowledge that God grants health, provision, and abundance, we can be generous with the gifts with which we have been entrusted.

# 15

# The worst kind of lost

Now all the tax collectors and sinners were coming near to listen to him. And the Pharisees and the scribes were grumbling and saying, "This fellow welcomes sinners and eats with them." So he told them this parable: "Which one of you, having a hundred sheep and losing one of them, does not leave the ninety-nine in the wilderness and go after the one that is lost until he finds it?"

—Luke 15:1–4

Ever been lost? Ever been somewhere where nothing is familiar and there is no one to help?

It's a scary feeling to be lost, lonely, and vulnerable. Sheep have no natural defense when separated from the herd. Who is it that Christ refers to in this parable?

The lost sheep is each and every one of us at some point in our life, if only for a day, a week, or a short period of time. We have all strayed at some point. Being lost spiritually is the worst kind of lost. We oftentimes don't realize it has happened.

The world offers so much. There are the demands of work, family, a home, and much more. The world in which we live entices us and lures us away from God.

Our triune God searches and hunts for each of us relentlessly. Beckoning us to return to him. To return to our spiritual home.

# 16
## The meaningless pursuit of titles

But when you are invited, go and sit down at the lowest place, so that when your host comes, he may say to you, "Friend, move up higher," then you will be honored in the presence of all who sit at the table with you. For all who exalt themselves will be humbled, and those who humble themselves will be exalted.

—Luke 14:10–11

Christ spoke these words at the home of a Pharisee leader, after observing how the Pharisees took seats of honor at the table.

Christ took the opportunity to teach about the kingdom of God and discipleship, to challenge their pursuit of hollow titles and places of honor.

We need to invest in things that will last—faith, hope, love, a life lived well. Those things that will echo throughout eternity. Christians are called to be humble, which does not mean being a punching bag or doormat.

It is about being honest with yourself about who you are, and owning that we all make mistakes. It's about admitting that we're all broken and that there is only one way to fix that—through faith, through the cross, and through Christ.

# 17
# Many talents, one body

For just as the body is one and has many members, and all the members of the body, though many, are one body, so it is with Christ. For in the one Spirit we were all baptized into one body—Jews or Greeks, slaves or free—and we were all made to drink of one Spirit.

—1 Corinthians 12:12–13

What is the church? Four walls, a roof, and a place to go on Sunday? A place where we go through the same rituals every time we meet?

The church is far more than that. The church is the living, breathing body of Christ.

It is one body with many distinct parts, made up of talented people who have answered the call God has placed on their lives.

The church has to reach out into the community, seeking out the lost and marginalized.

The church has to be passionate, vibrant, and bold if we seek to make disciples of Jesus Christ with the hope of transforming the world.

# 18

# Our most authentic self is found in Christ

We know that our old self was crucified with him so that the body of sin might be destroyed, and we might no longer be enslaved to sin. For whoever has died is freed from sin. But if we have died with Christ, we believe that we will also live with him.

—Romans 6:6–8

You are not defined by how much you make, the home you live in, or the things that you do. You are not defined by how well you can throw, kick, or hit a ball. You are much more than that. You are not the mistakes you've made, the people you've upset, or the dreams that went unfulfilled.

Who you are at the very core of your being—your most authentic, genuine, and comfortable-in-your-own-skin self—is found in faith. It is found with God, and it is found in Christ's sacrifice on the cross.

True identity is always found in faith. Young, old, graduates, everyone. The only lasting, authentic identity that exists is in the knowledge that you're a child of God—first, foremost, and forever.

# 19
# Everything starts with prayer

Then Jesus told them a parable about their need to pray always and not to lose heart. He said, "In a certain city there was a judge who neither feared God nor had respect for people. In that city there was a widow who kept coming to him and saying, 'Grant me justice against my oppressors.' For a while he refused; but later he said to himself, 'Though I have no fear of God and no respect for anyone, yet because this widow keeps bothering me, I will grant her justice, so that she may not wear me out by continually coming.'"

—Luke 18:1–5

Christ tells his disciples about their constant need for prayer, to show them that they must never give up. What is your constant prayer?

Christ tells the parable of the persistent widow to illustrate his point. A widow relentlessly asks for justice from a judge unlikely to give it. She continues with her request; she perseveres and doesn't give up. She wears the judge down, and he grants her request.

How fortunate are we to have a righteous, merciful, loving, and fair judge? How fortunate are we to know that the stain of sin, all the bad things we've done and silly things we've said, are not held against us?

Prayer is important, prayer works, and prayer heals. Everything starts with prayer. God welcomes our prayers, petitions, and requests. Prayer is powerful. Prayer brings peace. What is your constant prayer?

# 20
# Making it right

Jesus answered, "My kingdom is not from this world. If my kingdom were from this world, my followers would be fighting to keep me from being handed over to the Jews. But as it is, my kingdom is not from here." Pilate asked him, "So you are a king?" Jesus answered, "You say that I am a king. For this I was born, and for this I came into the world, to testify to the truth. Everyone who belongs to the truth listens to my voice." Pilate asked him, "What is truth?"

—John 18:36–38

Good Friday, can you imagine? I'm one guy trying to figure life out, and I've done some pretty bad things. There are approximately 7.5 billion people on the face of this planet, some doing good things and others doing things that aren't so nice. That is a lot of sin to take on. The cup of suffering that Christ had to drink. The worst of the worst—starvation, torture, exploitation, human trafficking, sexual assault, loneliness, rejection, and abandonment, to name only a few.

He had to take on God's dislike and wrath for sin and make it right. He stood in the gap that existed between us and God, and he bridged it. He made it right. Don't you just love it when someone makes something right? He made it right when one of his disciples betrayed him for thirty pieces of silver and when one of those closest to him denied him three times. He stayed true to his mission through an unjust trial and in spite of the physical abuse he had to endure.

"What is truth?" Pontius Pilate asked Christ. The truth stood right in front of him. I hope through this mystery of faith that you would know in your heart that Christ made it right, and that he treasures you for who you are and isn't concerned about what you are not.

# 21
## The proof of the resurrection

Now on the same day two of them were going to a village called Emmaus about seven miles from Jerusalem, and talking with each other about all these things that had happened. While they were talking and discussing, Jesus himself came near and went with them, but their eyes were kept from recognizing him.

—Luke 24:13–16

Christ had been nailed to a cross, died, and buried in a tomb. His disciples were dejected. All seemed to be lost. What would they do now?

Two of them were walking to Emmaus, a village outside of Jerusalem. Christ joined them, but they didn't know it was him. That happens often. We are lonely, upset, dealing with grief over the loss of a loved one or our own mortality—and we find that Christ is walking alongside us.

For forty days after the resurrection, Christ walked with his disciples to help convince them of his bodily resurrection. As difficult, cold, and final as death seems, it should be celebrated by people of faith. It hurts to see loved ones pass and to live without them. But there is victory in death, the celebration of eternal life.

# 22
# Place your trust in God

Don't let your hearts be troubled. Believe in God, believe also in me. In my Father's house there are many dwelling places. If it were not so, would I have told you that I go to prepare a place for you?

—John 14:1–2

The fourteenth chapter of John is one of my favorites and, I would contend, one of the richest chapters in all of scripture. The first few verses provide comfort to those grieving the loss of a loved one: "Don't be troubled, trust God. In my Father's house there are many rooms, and I am going to prepare a place for you ... When everything is ready, I will come and get you so that you will always be with me." Christ follows those comforting words with "I am the way, the truth, and the life. No one can come to the Father except through me."

I think Christ's statement—"I am the way, the truth, and the life"—cuts to the very core of the Gospel and speaks to the man that he was. Christ came to this world to erase the stain of sin and to bridge the divide it caused. Christ is the truth that Pontius Pilate studied as he negotiated with himself what to do with this man they called the King of the Jews. The Christian life is full, rich, and selfless. It is where our most authentic self meets our greatest joy. Christ is the way, the truth, and the life.

# 23

# We must take time to pray to meet the demands of this life

In the morning, while it was still very dark, he got up and went out to a deserted place, and there he prayed. And Simon and his companions hunted for him. When they found him, they said to him, "Everyone is searching for you." He answered them, "Let us go on to the neighboring towns, so that I may proclaim the message there also; for that is what I came out to do."

—Mark 1:35–38

Ever wondered why Christ got up early to pray? Christ calmed a storm when the boat he and his disciples were in started to fill with water and those in it were freaking out. As he reaches the shoreline and steps onto land, Christ is met by a man who has demons. I wonder if Christ thought, *You know, I just got out of the boat. Can I have a minute to myself?* Have you ever walked in the door after a rough day at work, only to be met with a barrage of requests or demands?

The demands on Christ were incredible. The demands of work, family, home, church, and the activities of our children can be exhausting. We have to find time to be in prayer. We have to be reminded of its power and the peace that it brings. Do you know what happens when we encounter Christ in prayer? Life changes, light enters, and transformation occurs.

# 24
# Faith calls us to sacrifice

To another he said, "Follow me." But he said, "Lord, first let me go and bury my father." But Jesus said to him, "Let the dead bury their own dead; but as for you, go and proclaim the kingdom of God." Another said, "I will follow you, Lord; but let me first say farewell to those at my home." Jesus said to him, "No one who puts a hand to the plow and looks back is fit for the kingdom of God."

—Luke 9:59–62

On the surface, this parable Christ spoke is confusing and maybe a little harsh. There are many levels to his words, and his parables weren't for only a cursory look. Anything worth accomplishing or fighting for takes effort and time. Our faith is no different. Christ is talking about the sacrifice that has to be made to follow him. He doesn't pull any punches on what it entails.

Faith doesn't consist of occasional worship attendance and prayer. Scripture has to be studied, wrestled with, and discussed. The depths of God, his love, and our souls are a mystery. There is so much depth that we may not discover all of it in this lifetime. It takes time, effort, and investment, but God reveals himself to us along the journey. The more we know about God, the greater knowledge we gain of ourselves.

# 25

## To whom have you shown mercy?

But wanting to justify himself, he asked Jesus, "And who is my neighbor?" Jesus replied, "A man was going down to Jerusalem to Jericho, and fell into the hands of robbers, who stripped him, beat him and went away, leaving him half dead."

—Luke 10:29–30

Who is your neighbor? That is the question from the often-quoted parable of the good Samaritan. This question may or may not be about the people who live close to you and work with you. How do we treat people who are different from us? The Samaritans were a racially mixed bunch who sometimes worshipped pagan gods. They weren't pure and holy.

A man traveling to Jericho falls into the hands of robbers, who strip and beat him, leaving him half dead alongside the road. A priest passes by and moves to the other side of the road. A Levite, one who serves in the temple, passes by and does the same. A Samaritan passes by and has compassion for the beaten man. He does more than help—he goes all out. He cares for the injured man as if he were family. The Samaritan bandages his wounds, finds him shelter, and pays for the man to stay with him. "Take care of him," the Samaritan tells the innkeeper, "and I will pay whatever it costs."

Sound familiar? Christ thought of each of us and said the same thing: "I will pay whatever it costs."

# 26

# What will become of the church?

After this the Lord appointed seventy others and sent them on ahead of him in pairs to every town and place where he himself intended to go. He said to them, "The harvest is plentiful, but the laborers are few; therefore ask the Lord of the harvest to send out laborers into his harvest."

—Luke 10:1–2

The harvest is plentiful, but the laborers are few. Why is the church in decline? Why do so few people have the time for church? People are too busy, and church is inconvenient and only for old people. It is antiquated, and there is too much this world has to offer to be bothered with it.

It is our job as followers of Christ to bring the gospel to people, invite them to church, and live a life of service.

There is an emptiness that exists within each of us that can be properly filled only by faith. The problem is that too many people try to fill it with hundreds of television channels, social media, video games, too many activities, and chasing after the wind. That emptiness or feeling of being incomplete can be filled only by God.

# 27
# Are you Mary or Martha?

Now as they went on their way, he entered a certain village, where a woman named Martha welcomed him into her home. She had a sister named Mary, who sat at the Lord's feet and listened to what he was saying. But Martha was distracted by her many tasks; so she came to him and asked, "Lord, do you not care that my sister has left me to do all the work by myself? Tell her then to help me."

—Luke 10:38–40

Christ and his disciples stop in the town of Bethany to visit Mary, Martha, and Lazarus. Christ is making his final journey to Jerusalem. Martha is feverishly preparing a meal and getting things in order. Where is her sister Mary? She is at Christ's feet, fully present with him, listening to him teach and preach.

Martha's frustration boils over: "Lord, do you not care that my sister has left me to do all the work by myself? Tell her to help me." But Christ corrects her and says, "Martha, you are worried and distracted by many things, but there is need of only one thing. Mary has chosen the better part, which will not be taken from her."

Are you Mary or Martha? Too many times we find ourselves like Martha—hurried, anxious, and frustrated. We need time to be like Mary, fully present with our God. In a busy world with busy people and crazy schedules, take time to be like Mary.

# 28
# Father, holy and blessed be thy name

He was praying in a certain place, and after he had finished, one of his disciples said to him, "Lord, teach us to pray, as John taught his disciples." He said to them, "When you pray, say: Father, hallowed be your name. Your kingdom come. Give us each day our daily bread. And forgive us or sins, for we ourselves forgive everyone indebted to us. And do not bring us to the time of trial."

—Luke 11:1–4

Jesus went to be in prayer. He did this often. He rose early to pray, or he went to the mountain to pray, or he prayed and was transfigured, or … Always praying, but why?

When his disciples ask Christ for guidance on how to pray, Christ responds, "Father, hallowed be your name. Your kingdom come. Give us each day our daily bread. Forgive us our sins, for we ourselves forgive everyone indebted to us. And do not bring us to the time of trial."

This is the basis or foundation for the Lord's Prayer. Petitions for provision, forgiveness, and God's kingdom here on earth. Sometimes prayer seems clumsy and awkward. Sometimes we don't know what to pray for, but that's okay. The acknowledgement and dialogue with our Creator is the important part. He knows the condition of our hearts.

# 29
## Every day is a battle

It happened, late one afternoon, when David rose from his couch and was walking about on the roof of the king's house that he saw from the roof a woman bathing; the woman was very beautiful.

—2 Samuel 11:2

Every day is a battle. Emotional, physical, and spiritual ground is won or lost. Reputations, careers, marriages, and families aren't torn down overnight, but over time. King David was a man after God's own heart. David respected Saul's leadership in spite of Saul's attempts to kill him. God granted David many victories in battle, he became famous, and he became king.

In a season of battle, David stays home to rest. He sees a woman of unusual beauty bathing. Lust consumes him, and he has to have her. In a short time, Bathsheba will be pregnant with his child, and her husband will die as David tries to cover his tracks. The child conceived dies shortly after birth.

Every day is a battle, so guard your heart always. Understand that lust, greed, envy, and jealousy may be just around the corner.

# 30
# We remember those who gave

So if you have been raised with Christ, seek the things that are above, where Christ is, seated at the right hand of God. Set your minds on things that are above, not on things that are on earth, for you have died, and your life is hidden with Christ in God. When Christ who is your life is revealed, then you also will be revealed with him in glory.

—Colossians 3:1–4

How do you want to be remembered? We have to accept that death is a part of this life. Not to be feared, but to be a celebration of this life and the life to come. From a jail cell, Paul wrote, "For you have died and your life is hid with Christ in God." The person you were before coming to faith is gone, and you have been born again. When that happens, life changes.

Lives that burned for the things of this world are transformed into selfless lives of service. Things are seen for what they are. They have functional value and it's nice to have nice things, but not at the expense of being able to do for others or finding your self-worth in material possessions.

We don't remember people for what they took—we remember people for what they gave. How do you want to be remembered?

# 31

# You are first and foremost a child of God

Now large crowds were traveling with him; and he turned and said to them, "Whoever comes to me and does not hate father and mother, wife and children, brothers and sisters, yes, and even life itself, cannot be my disciple."

—Luke 14:25–26

"Whoever comes to me and does not hate his father and mother, wife and children, brothers and sisters, and even life itself, cannot be my disciple." Why would Christ say something so inflammatory and over the top? He surely doesn't mean that, does he?

Christ made sure that he had the attention of those who followed him and became his disciples. The word *hate* in biblical times didn't have the same meaning as it does today. It did not mean an intense dislike, but to love one thing less than another.

"Nothing is more important than my kids and my family!" I understand. I think the takeaway from this scripture is that first and foremost, you are a precious child of God. Too often we forget that about ourselves and others. Too quick to assess, judge, and condemn. First, foremost, and forever, you are a child of God. It's not about disliking your family, but about loving God even more.

# 32

# We serve a big God

Do not fear, for I am with you, do not be afraid, for I am your God; I will strengthen you, I will help you, I will uphold you with my victorious right hand.

—Isaiah 41:10

"Fear not, do not be afraid," Christ said. He talked about fear often. Fear can be terrible. It paralyzes and can keep God's people from being about God's work. Thomas Merton said, "Fear is spiritual immaturity." We shrink and denigrate our God when we fear. Fear would be far less common if we turned to God in our time of need. When our circumstances overwhelm us, when there isn't enough money to pay the bills, or when we obsess over everything that might happen. How many times have you lain awake at night with your mind racing?

We serve a big God. We need to be reminded that we serve a big God. We serve a God so big, merciful, loving, and just that he came to this world to live with us and taught us how to live. He died so that we wouldn't have to. With a God like that, what is there to fear?

# 33

## How will your story of faith read?

By faith Abraham obeyed when he was called to set out to a place that he was to receive as an inheritance; and he set out, not knowing where he was going. By faith he stayed for a time in the land he had been promised, as in a foreign land, living in tents, as did Isaac and Jacob, who were heirs with him of the same promise.

—Hebrews 11:8–9

It was by faith that Abraham obeyed God. It was by faith that Abel offered a more acceptable sacrifice to God. It was by faith that Moses was hidden by his parents after his birth. They knew there was something special about this child. By faith. How will your "by faith" read? It was by faith … What will you do?

It was by faith that Moses decided not to be part of the royal Egyptian family. Instead he shared in the oppression of God's people, the Hebrew slaves. Moses wasn't a saint. He struck and killed an Egyptian, then fled for his life.

It was by faith, and a lot of reassurance from God, that Moses returned to Egypt to lead the Hebrews to the Promised Land. Pharaoh increased their work, and the Israelites would not listen to him. By faith, Moses persevered. It took several plagues and the Passover to set the Israelites free.

God can do a lot through a person of faith. Moses had struck a man down and wasn't an eloquent speaker. Only Christ's and David's names appear more often than Moses's in the Bible. How will your "by faith" read?

# 34
# God prepares us while we wait

A certain man was ill, Lazarus of Bethany, the village of Mary and her sister Martha. Mary was the one who anointed the Lord with perfume and wiped his feet with her hair; her brother Lazarus was ill. So the sisters sent a message to Jesus, "Lord, he whom you love is ill." But when Jesus heard it, he said, "This illness does not lead to death; rather it is for God's glory, so that the Son of God may be glorified through it."

—John 11:1–4

When Jesus's friend Lazarus becomes ill and is near death, Mary and Martha send word to Jesus of the situation. And Jesus rushes to Lazarus's side to save him? No, he doesn't. He waits.

How do you deal with waiting? How do you deal with God's "Not yet"? I don't like to wait. I am very impatient. I get mad and frustrated when things don't happen at the speed I want them to. But God's chosen ones, including Christ, had to wait. They had their own "not yet" moments. Many times waiting is the furnace that burns the dross from our souls. Much can be learned from waiting if we turn to God during that time.

When Jesus arrived in Bethany, he was told that Lazarus had been dead for days. "Didn't I tell you that you will see God's glory if you believe?" Christ asked. Didn't I tell you that you will see God's glory if you believe Lazarus is raised from the dead? We will too. We will see God's glory by our belief in him.

# 35

# Earth or eternity, convenience or Christ

There was a rich man who was dressed in purple and fine linen and who feasted sumptuously every day. And at his gate lay a poor man named Lazarus, covered with sores, who longed to satisfy his hunger with what fell from the rich man's table; even the dogs would come and lick his sores.

—Luke 16:19–21

A rich man had everything that money could buy, that his flesh could want. Every day was a day to indulge. At his gate lay a poor beggar named Lazarus, who longed for the scraps that fell from the rich man's table. Lazarus had no one and nothing. His existence was so miserable that wild dogs would come and lick his sores. The rich man could have easily helped him, but he chose not to.

Both men died. The roles were reversed. The beggar, Lazarus, was carried by the angels to his eternal reward of heaven. The rich man wasn't as fortunate. His way of living earned him a fast pass through the gates of hell. The rich man became the beggar, begging for Lazarus to give him a few drops of water because he was in anguish in these flames.

Abraham said, "Remember during your lifetime you had everything and Lazarus had nothing. A great chasm divides us."

A great chasm divides us. A great chasm begins to form when we pick earthly things over eternity, convenience over Christ—and subsequently, hell over heaven. Let us do for one another out of the abundance that God has granted each of us.

# 36
# Immanuel, God with us

Remember Jesus Christ, raised from the dead, a descendant of David—that is my gospel, for which I suffer hardship, even to the point of being chained like a criminal. But the word of God is not chained.

—2 Timothy 2:8–9

Never forget Jesus Christ. If only those words were repeated constantly in our minds, woven into the fabric of our souls, and became the way we saw the world. Too many times I get caught up in the desires of my own flesh. What is it to never forget Jesus?

Jesus came to this earth with all the frailty of an infant, born in a stable. He had to be protected from a jealous king who wanted him dead. A man, fully divine and fully human, who dealt with the everyday things that we have to deal with–frustration, rejection, temptation, and abandonment.

What kind of God allows the very people he came to save to beat him relentlessly and mercilessly, scourging and ripping his flesh? A merciful, righteous, and loving God. A living God who loves far beyond what we can imagine.

# 37
# Faith, family, and forgiveness

Husbands, love your wives, just as Christ loved the church and gave himself up for her, in order to make her holy by cleansing her with the washing of water by the word, so as to present the church to himself in splendor, without a spot or wrinkle or anything of the kind—yes, so that she may be holy and without blemish.

—Ephesians 5:25–27

Faith, family, forgiveness. If the church doesn't offer anything different from what the world offers, why do people go? In a world, culture, and society where almost everything is focused on the individual and their rights, the church has to be different. Faith, family, and forgiveness.

Within a family or in community, some—not all, but some—of the rights of the individual are sacrificed for the good of the whole. The needs of others are taken into account and given priority, and we try to meet those needs as best as we can.

This flesh screams its need for retaliation when injured or harmed, demands better treatment, and wants its own way far too often. An unwillingness to forgive is heavy and leads to bitterness. Forgiveness frees both those who injure and the injured. As Christians, we are called to live out our faith, treat each other like family, and always be willing to forgive.

# 38
# Restoration and healing

Therefore thus says the Lord of hosts, "Because you have not obeyed my words, I am going to send for all the tribes of the north," says the Lord, "even for King Nebuchadnezzar of Babylon, my servant, and I will bring them against this land and its inhabitants, and against all these nations around."

—Jeremiah 25:8–9

Under the rule of King Nebuchadnezzar, the Babylonians destroyed the city, destroyed the temple, and killed its leaders. Then they took with them the more talented Jews to live in exile. God's city, God's temple, and God's people were seemingly conquered—downtrodden, defeated, and discouraged. We've all been there, and some never leave. It is as if the whole weight of the world is fixed on our shoulders.

Redemption, restoration, and healing. We are all in need of it, but do we acknowledge it or see it that way? Be tough. Don't cry. It's a long way from your heart. You're fine! Keep limping along; someday you won't feel anything. Negative emotions that aren't dealt with can resurface as anxiety, depression, alcohol/drug addiction, and many other unhealthy things.

With God's help and direction, Nehemiah and Ezra organized the effort to rebuild the city of Jerusalem. God offers the same restoration and healing today. We need to admit our brokenness, express our need and want for healing, and allow the Great Physician to begin his work.

# 39
# Listening to our lives

And James and John, the sons of Zebedee, came forward to him, and said to him, "Teacher, we want you to do for us whatever we ask of you." And he said to them, "What do you want me to do for you?" "Grant us to sit, one at your right hand and one at your left, in your glory."

—Mark 10:35–37

"Give us seats of honor, one at your right and the other at your left," James and John, two of Christ's disciples, asked of him. They had no idea what they were asking for. "Can ye drink of the cup that I drink of?" Christ asks. The cup of suffering, sorrow, sin, rejection, torture, and the worst experience you've had times a hundred, maybe a thousand.

What is in your cup? The joy of family, friends, and faith? A life lived well. But what about the heavy stuff at the bottom? The stuff that only a few people might know of? Brokenness, isolation, grief, divorce, anxiety, and abandonment, to name a few. Feelings of emptiness. There are times I feel empty. It is a sad and lonely place. I try to avoid it; we all do.

We need those times of silence and brokenness to bring us closer to God. Only God can fill and heal those places within us. We must be willing to look and listen to our own lives. To ask God for healing in those places that haunt us.

# 40

## Doing for those who can't do anything for us

Most of what the world offers is conditional. You go to school to earn a diploma or a degree. You go to work to earn a paycheck. Goods and services are exchanged for money.

Each one is conditioned or dependent on the other. If we're not careful, this bleeds into our relationships. If I do this for you, I expect this in return. I helped you, so now you are obligated to help me. As Christians, we are called to be unconditional people.

We don't define the worth of people by what they can or cannot do. It doesn't matter what someone earns or how much education they have. We must be able to do for others without expecting anything in return. This is difficult, and I struggle with it. Our relationships become shallow when they are conditional.

We are called to be deep and loving people, to love and do for others who may not be able to do anything for us.

# 41
# Suffering gives us a choice

Christ is teaching in the synagogue on the Sabbath. A crippled woman comes to hear him preach. She hasn't been able to stand up straight for the past eighteen years, but where do you find her? Worshipping God. Can you imagine that bad back, hip or ankle, or migraine headache plaguing you for eighteen years?

It's awful when we can't do the things that we want to. In a world where speed and efficiency are king, little time is left to be on the sidelines.

The hurt, harm, and injuries that we suffer in this life give us a choice. We can run to God or away from him. We can embrace faith or turn our back on it. We can choose to get better or find resentment and bitterness.

Anything that causes us to suffer presents us with a choice. God loves us enough to let us choose what to do with him. God loves us enough to heal those places that hurt deep within us. Christ saw this woman's suffering and set her free from it. He can do the same for you.

# 42

# Prayer works, and God still listens

Prayer. The people in the Bible cried out to God. David, in the Psalms, and Samuel's mother, Hannah, are two examples. They didn't hold anything back.

Life is messy, but I present prayer that is neat, clean, and sanitized. Clean, composed prayer. Putting on our Sunday best for Sunday school and church. Does presenting ourselves at our best make us more acceptable to God? It does not. It doesn't matter what people wear to church, as long as they are there.

Most of what I've heard in my time in church is kind, warm, and fuzzy prayer. It doesn't often happen that we cry out and allow ourselves to be vulnerable in front of others. Hannah was barren, a source of shame and embarrassment in biblical times. She cried out to God and promised to dedicate her child to him. So God granted her prayer, and Hannah kept her promise.

Many of us know Samuel's story. Pray with zest, pray with all your heart, pray your most authentic prayer. Prayer works. God still listens.

# 43
## Our guilt, Christ's sacrifice

"What is your charge against this man?" Pontius Pilate asks.

"We wouldn't have handed him over to you if he weren't a criminal!" the religious leaders respond.

Christ was guilty. Guilty of preaching, teaching, and healing. Guilty of challenging the brand of religion that did not set people free. Guilty of calling out those Pharisees on their arrogance, their many rules and unwillingness to help people in need.

Guilty. I'm guilty. Probably you are, too. Guilty of being selfish, apathetic, and unwilling to help at times. I'm guilty of far worse. The darkness that lies within me is not something of which I'm proud. None of us are. We didn't ask for it—we inherited it.

The conviction of sin that God has placed on me should keep me humble, but it doesn't stop this flesh from rebelling and wanting its own way. Christ took on our guilt so that we wouldn't have to carry its weight. He met death head-on and conquered it, so that it couldn't touch us. Christ was the spotless, sinless sacrifice that set us free from our sin, guilt, and shame.

# 44
# The heart of discipleship

Christ had been baptized by John the Baptist, tempted in the desert, and selected his twelve disciples. With crowds following him, he went up to a mountain overlooking the Sea of Galilee and delivered the Beatitudes.

The paradox of Christian faith. Empty yourself in order to be filled. Those who are humble will be exalted. You have to be last in order to be first. Christ turned the expectations of the culture and society of his time, and ours, on their heads.

"Blessed are the poor in spirit." Being poor in spirit doesn't mean the absence of spirituality, but an utter dependence on God. This first petition is the beginning of discipleship. Disciples understand their own brokenness and put Christ, the cross, and faith at the center of their lives. Blessed are those who come before God with open hearts, open minds, and empty hands. "Blessed are the poor in spirit, for theirs is the kingdom of heaven."

# 45
# Surrender

Advent. A season of expectation, anticipation, and longing. Longing for deliverance from the sin and evil of this world. Advent is also a time of preparation and patience. We have to wait on God's perfect timing. We have to wait on God when we don't understand and it doesn't make any sense.

It can be difficult to surrender to God and his timing when it doesn't align with our own.

This is difficult. I'd like to tell you that I have this figured out, but I haven't. My ability to surrender and my living sacrifice crawls off the altar ten seconds after I place it there. I'll surrender or wait patiently under these conditions—as long as I can live comfortably and do what I want for the most part. It doesn't work that way.

Faith is the only context in which our lives make any sense. Surrender is at the heart of Christian faith. While you wait, if you are in your own season of Advent, surrender your heart to God.

# 46
# I want, I want

For those who live according to the flesh set their minds on the things of the flesh, but those who live according to the Spirit set their minds on the things of the Spirit. To set the mind on the flesh is death, but to set the mind on the Spirit is life and peace.

—Romans 8:5-6

How the world could be changed if we did what Paul writes of—setting our mind on the Spirit. We ascend into the spiritual world, but our flesh pulls us back. How much conflict is created on all levels because someone had to have his or her own way?

I do this all the time. I want to sit down and watch what I want to watch on television. I want to eat at the restaurant at which I want to eat. I want my children to be great at an activity, even more than they do, so I put way too much pressure on them.

If we could only bridle the "I want …" We can. It is possible through faith, through Christ and his sacrifice on the cross. He showed us what it looks like to be selfless.

# 47
## The wages of sin

And if your foot causes you to stumble, cut it off; it is better for you to enter life lame than to have two feet and to be thrown into hell. And if your eye causes you to stumble, tear it out; it is better for you to enter the kingdom of God with one eye than to have two eyes and to be thrown into hell.

—Mark 9:45–47

Christ didn't hold anything back when talking about discipleship to those who would follow him. I don't think Christ wants us to mutilate our bodies.

He was very clear about the power of sin and the measures we have to take to guard against it. Cutting off your foot or plucking out an eye is extreme, but there are areas of weakness within us that cause us to sin.

The need for approval or affirmation is oftentimes sought in dangerous areas. Impulsiveness, attention seeking, and coveting are all too real. Bright and shiny material possessions can dazzle our eyes and make their way into our hearts if we are not careful.

# 48
# The word became flesh

In the beginning was the word, and the world was with God, and the word was God.

—John 1:1

These words are poetic, beautiful, and awe inspiring. The three persons of the Trinity are interlocked as only spiritual beings can be.

Not limited by time and space, those things in which we humans are trapped, God's truth has existed since the beginning of time. That truth was revealed to us in the flesh as Jesus the Christ. The word became flesh.

Why would God empty himself of his divinity to live as a poor carpenter and die a criminal's death? A God who loves. A God who *is* love. If I could only love a fraction of that. What love I have seems incomplete.

# 49
# The danger of judging others

Therefore you have no excuse, whoever you are, when you judge another, for in passing judgment on another you condemn yourself, because you, the judge, are doing the very same things.

—Romans 2:1

Judging others is so easy that it seems natural. Loving them and taking the time to know their story is far more difficult.

I venture to say that if we truly knew each other and lived in community, there would be far more compassion and understanding than judgment. It seems like the world has strayed from the concept of community, from knowing and engaging each other often on deep and meaningful levels.

Neighbors scarcely know those who live near them at times.

We weren't made to judge one another; we were made to love one another. Judging others reflects on the one who judges.

# 50
# Do we know how to suffer?

And not only that, but we also boast in our sufferings, knowing that suffering produces endurance, and endurance produces character, and character produces hope.

—Romans 5:3–4

Suffering is part of this life, but do we know how to suffer well? Have we had any instruction? Do our children understand that there will be times of loneliness, grief, and emptiness?

Hopes and dreams that weren't attained in spite of gallant efforts. I think many people do not know how to suffer. I struggle with it myself. Unfulfilling jobs and careers, relationships that end in separation or divorce, and always thinking the grass is greener somewhere else.

Even though we suffer, we have far more to celebrate. There are so many things that we oftentimes take for granted—good health, family, provisions, shelter, friends, comfort, and the list goes on. Pray during your time and season of suffering, knowing that God will strengthen you and give you hope.

# 51
# Offering ourselves as a living sacrifice

I appeal to you therefore, brothers and sisters, by the mercies of God, to present your bodies as a living sacrifice, holy and acceptable to God, which is your spiritual worship.

—Romans 12:1

As a pastor, it can be difficult to get people to attend church regularly, let alone ask them to sacrifice their lives. It is only by the grace of God that we enjoy good health, shelter, provision, family, and the endless list of things with which we have been blessed.

Sacrificing for God our time, talent, money, and our lives should come easily. But it doesn't seem to work that way. This flesh is selfish.

We must ascend into the spiritual world in order to offer ourselves as a living sacrifice, holy and acceptable to God.

# 52

# Coming before God with empty hands and an open heart

Blessed are the poor in spirit, for theirs is the kingdom of heaven.

—Matthew 5:3

In what was one of Christ's first sermons, he delivered the Beatitudes.

Christ's parables were not designed to be gently passed over. They have to be studied and wrestled with. Poverty of spirit is the petition on which all others rely. It doesn't refer to the lack of spirituality. It is an utter dependence on God, not on ourselves.

Being convicted of our sin, owning our brokenness, and putting Christ, the cross, and faith at the center of our lives. We've all strayed from God, if only for a season. My living sacrifice crawls off the altar ten seconds after I place it there.

Blessed are those who come before God with open hearts, open minds, and empty hands.

# 53
# Those with hearts of faith grieve

Blessed are those that mourn, for they will be comforted.

—Matthew 5:4

Unfortunately, the world gives us reminders of what some people are capable of. Those who see with eyes or hearts of faith feel the pain of those who suffer. They empathize and sympathize with people who are lost, hungry, tired, and cold.

People take life in the name of their own religion, political campaigns throw verbal daggers at each other, children starve, and refugees flee from war-torn countries. Life is sacred and to be honored. Too many times it is treated as if it has little value.

We mourn our own sin-filled existence and thank Christ for rescuing us from it. It is only by the grace of God that each of us is as fortunate as we are. Hearts filled with faith grieve and are called to action to alleviate the suffering of people less fortunate. One day, those who mourn will be comforted.

# 54

# Blessed are those who are humble

Blessed are the meek, for they will inherit the earth.

—Matthew 5:5

Blessed, or fortunate, are those humble in heart, for they will inherit the earth. Oftentimes God has to introduce pain into our lives in order to bring us closer to him.

This flesh can find pride quickly.

The victories that God has granted us can be quickly taken credit for. Those who are humble know their own sin and their need to be saved from it.

Those who turn to faith, those who know Christ and his sacrifice on the cross, will inherit the earth.

# 55
## Those who pursue holiness

Blessed are those who hunger and thirst for righteousness, for they will be filled.

—Matthew 5:6

Blessed are those who pursue holiness, for they will be filled. Each of us, regardless of the bad stuff we've done, has the image of the Creator within us.

Divinity lives and breathes within our souls. That divinity longs to be reunited with the One who placed it there. It pulls at us, that emptiness within us that can be filled only by God's presence.

People who pursue God, who are on the journey to sanctification, are filled with the fruits of the Spirit.

# 56

# No one exists outside God's mercy and grace

Blessed are the merciful, for they will receive mercy.

—Matthew 5:7

We all need to be shown mercy and grace. It is only through God's grace that we are saved and exempt from the punishment we would otherwise deserve.

We are called to extend that same grace to others. God's unlimited treasure of this thing called grace saved Paul from a lifetime of persecuting Christians and made him one of the New Testament's greatest authors.

No one lives outside of God's grace and mercy. No one. Not you, not your neighbor, not that person at work you can't stand. When we show mercy to others, we model the one who created everything and everyone.

# 57

# Christ convicts us of our sin

You have heard that it was said, "You shall not murder" and "Whoever murders shall be liable to judgment." But I say to you that if you are angry with a brother or sister, you will be liable to judgment; and if you insult a brother or sister, you will be liable to the council; and if you say, "You fool," you will be liable to the fire of hell.

—Matthew 5:21–22

Anger is a powerful emotion. It is easy to get swept up and away with it. Things are said that are regretted later. Decisions are made that have long-lasting ramifications.

I've held myself in higher esteem than those who have taken the life of another. But Christ levels the playing field.

Mere anger with a brother or sister, not assault or murder, but anger alone is equated with murder. Anger can be productive if harnessed and channeled. Christ convicts us of our sin, even when we compare it with something we think is far more offensive.

Be quick to forgive someone of words spoken in anger. Don't forget to forgive yourself.

# 58
# Sins of the heart

You have heard that it was said, "You shall not commit adultery." But I say to you that everyone who looks at a woman with lust has already committed adultery with her in his heart.

—Matthew 5:27–28

It is easy for me to say that I've been faithful to my wife, not having had an extramarital affair. But when Christ says that anyone who looks on another woman with lust has committed adultery with her in his heart, I become very guilty.

Every day this happens to me. I'm not proud of it, but it is real. Christ knew how our eyes sometimes wander. My mind goes to those dark, carnal areas of wanting everything in its path.

This, and much more, is the reason we needed someone to save us from this ugliness, this thing called sin that ends in death. Christ meets us in our sin, convicts us, and then forgives us of it.

# 59
# Getting comfortable in our own skin

Ask and it will be given you; search, and you will find; knock, and the door will be opened for you. For everyone who asks receives, and everyone who searches finds, and for everyone who knocks, the door will be opened.

—Matthew 7:7–8

God's presence is everywhere, if we have eyes of faith to see it. In keeping with the paradox of faith, God's presence can also be hidden. Present and hidden?

Scripture tells us that those who are last will be first. Humble yourself in order to be exalted. I think that God wants us to pursue him. Going to church a couple of times and expecting to feel different probably won't work.

As we pursue and gain knowledge of God, we gain knowledge of ourselves. Both have depths that we may not reach in this life. Still, the more we seek and pursue God, the more comfortable we become in our own skin.

# 60
# Reaching in Christ's direction

Then suddenly a woman who had been suffering from hemorrhages for twelve years came up behind Jesus and touched the fringe of his cloak, for she said to herself, "If I only touch his cloak, I will be made well." Jesus turned, and seeing her he said, "Take heart, daughter; your faith has made you well."

—Matthew 9:20–22

Suffering is inevitable in this life. This woman had suffered for years, and to whom does she turn for healing? She turns to Christ. Not to alcohol, drugs, sex, or a witch doctor, nor does she immerse herself in work. She turns to Christ.

How much suffering could be alleviated if the people of this world did the same? In this example, physical healing took place by reaching out in Christ's direction.

Healing of old wounds, emotional and physical abuse, of not living up to the standards of others, and of failure is available as well. We only need to have faith and reach out to Christ.

# 61
# Anything but weak

Do not think that I have come to bring peace to the earth; I have not come to bring peace, but a sword. For I have come to set a man against his father, and a daughter against her mother, and a daughter-in-law against her mother-in-law; and one's foes will be members of one's own household.

—Matthew 10:34–36

Every day is a battle. Spiritual ground is won or lost every day. We can choose to spend time with our families and with other people or we can isolate and indulge ourselves. We can make the choice to add to our spiritual lives by living lives of discipline, or we can live for our flesh.

I think many people see Christ as being passive, but I don't. I see him as confrontational, consistently and boldly challenging the religious establishment.

As Christians, we are called to be kind and gentle, but not doormats or easy marks. We have conviction; we have principles and morals. Not to be obnoxious with, but to witness to our faith.

At any point during Christ's last hours, he could have stopped the trial, beating, and crucifixion. He chose not to. Not out of weakness, but out of obedience to his Father and out of his love for us.

# 62

# Take up your cross, deny yourself, and follow me

Then Jesus told his disciples, "If any want to become my followers, let them deny themselves and take up their cross and follow me. For those who want to save their life will lose it and those who lose their life for my sake will find it. For what will it profit them if they gain the whole world but forfeit their life? Or what will they give in return for their life?"

—Matthew 16:24–26

I preach often about being selfless and the giving of time, talent, and money. It is difficult to be selfless. The natural instinct of our human condition is to satisfy our wants and needs.

As I read about the lives of the saints, I am reminded of just how selfish I am. I want to watch *my* TV show and will leave the room if I can't. I go to great lengths to get out of things that I don't want to do. I want to do what I want to do when I want to do it. It's embarrassing.

"Take up your cross, deny yourself, and follow me." Take up your pain, sorrow, and suffering. Take up the disappointment, the times you felt rejected, abandoned, and alone. Nail all of it to the cross, deny yourself, and follow Christ. Separate the will of the flesh from the will of the Spirit. The flesh won't live forever—but the Spirit will.

# 63
# A childlike faith

At that time the disciples came to Jesus and asked, "Who is the greatest in the kingdom of heaven?" He called a child, whom he put among them, and said, "Truly I tell you, unless you change and become like children, you will never enter the kingdom of heaven. Whoever becomes humble like this child is the greatest in the kingdom of heaven. Whoever welcomes one such child in my name welcomes me."

—Matthew 18:1–4

The faith of a child. Most children don't have to worry about making mortgage payments, trying to keep the lights on, or providing for others.

Anxiety is a real problem in this day and age. I'd like to think that children don't occupy themselves with what might happen. Those are the worries of adults. Those worries are the sign of someone who needs to find a deeper level of faith—the faith of a child.

The faith that a child has in their parents is the faith we should have in our heavenly Father.

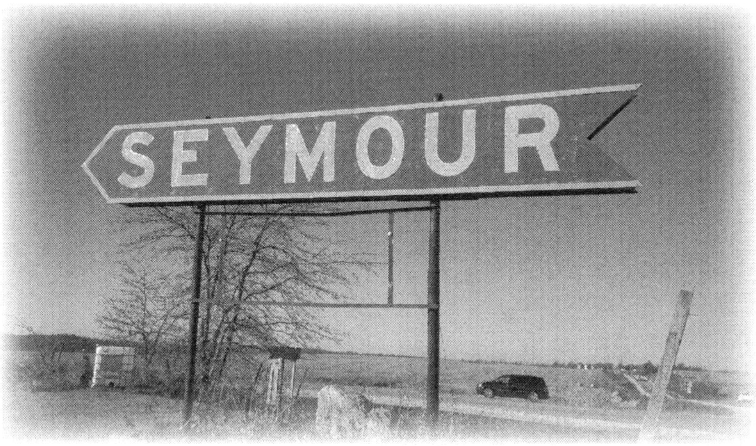
SEYMOUR

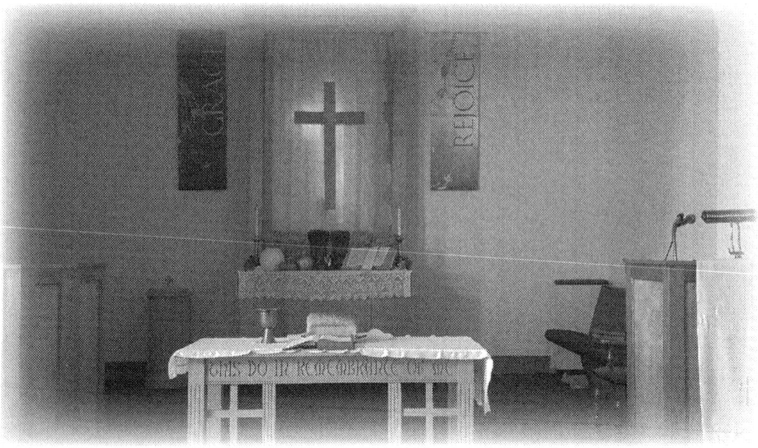
REJOICE
THIS DO IN REMEMBRANCE OF ME

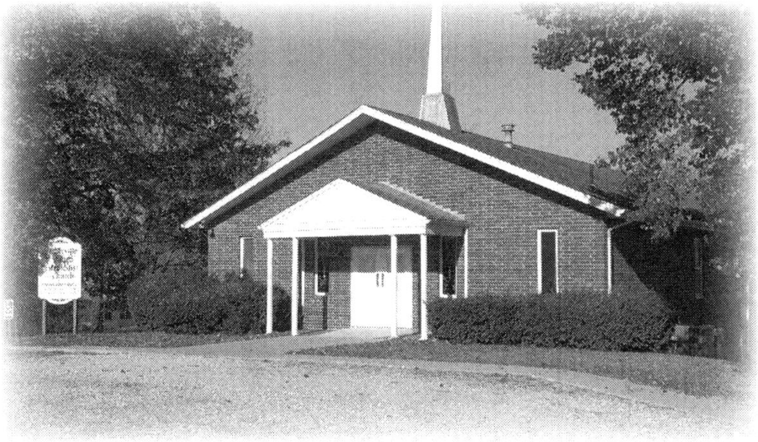

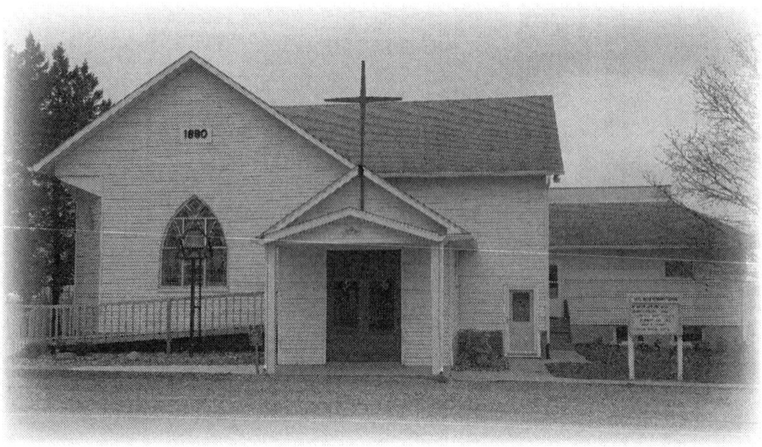
1890

# ABOUT THE AUTHOR

As with my call to ministry, I didn't have the credentials to do it, I felt that God was leading me put together this book of devotions. I hope this book adds to your spiritual journey. Shawn LaRue lives is Southeast Iowa with his wife and two sons. He has served the United Methodist Church in Seymour, Iowa, since July of 2015.

Made in the USA
Middletown, DE
22 March 2017